ESL – Glossary Edition: English-Arabic

S.T.E.M. Vocabulary for English Language Learners Who Speak ARABIC

Christine Canning-Wilson

Christine Canning Wilson / STEM ESL Arabic

ENGLISH TABLE OF CONTENTS

Christine Canning Wilson / STEM ESL Arabic

ENGLISH CORE WORDS USED IN SCIENCE, TECHNOLOGY, ENGINEERING AND MATH

for

ENGLISH LANGUAGE LEARNERS

IMPORTANT: The English Language has more words than your language. Some words may not have a translation. Some words are approximates. Some words are the same as the word in the English language. This book is only a guide. It will help you gain equity to the curriculum. Match the number in your language with the number used in the English Section. Ask your teacher for help.

English Language Vocabulary Lists

CLASSROOM INSTRUCTION VERBS USED IN SCIENCE, TECHNOLOGY, ENGINEERING, and MATH

1. Absorb

2. Accelerate

3. Action

4. Add

5. Align

6. Amplify

7. Analyze

8. Answer

9. Attach

10. Balance

11. Bring

12. To Change

13. Complete

14. Compute

15. Constant

16. Convert

17. Count

18. Decrease

19. Describe

20. Determine

21. Devise

22. Differentiate

23. Dilute

24. Displace

25. Do not touch

26. Drag

27. Engineering

28. Escape

29. Examine

30. Experiment

31. Evolve

32. Fix

33. Follow

34. Fracture

35. Gently handle

36. Glue

37. Grow

38. Guess

39. Heat

40. Hoist

41. Hold

42. Incomplete

43. Increase

44. Integrate

45. Leave

46. Lift

47. Lift

48. Listen

49. Lower

50. Measure

51. Mix

52. Multiply

53. Notice

54. Observe

55. Order

56. Partner

57. Place

58. Pour

59. Prohibited

60. Rank

61. Ration

62. Pound

63. Remove

64. Reaction

65. Read

66. Remove

67. Replace

68. Report

69. Rotate

70. Saturate

71. Science

72. To screw

73. Select

74. Simmer

75. Sort

76. Speak

77. Spill

78. Spin

79. State

80. Study

81. Subtract

82. Technology

83. Throw

84. Tie

85. To boil

86. Touch

87. To Transfer

88. Use

89. Write

90. Yield

SHAPES USED IN SCIENCE, TECHNOLOGY, ENGINEERING and MATH

1. Tube

2. Triangle

3. Cylinder

4. Cave

5. Arch

6. Circle

7. Square

8. Rectangle

9. Oval

10. Heart – Shaped

11. Wiggle

12. Circular

13. Wavy

14. Bump

15. Two dimensional

16. Three dimensional

17. Flat

18. Round

19. Cone

20. Parallel

21. Adjacent

22. Slit

SCIENCE VOCABULARY

23. A science project

24. Aberration

25. Absolute

26. Absorptive Power

27. Acceleration

28. Accelerator

29. Accelerometer

30. Accessory

31. Accommodation

32. Action

33. Adhesion

34. Adiabatic

35. Advantage

36. Aerial

37. Air Brake

38. Air Pump

39. Airplane

40. Algebra

41. Alternating Current

42. Alternation

43. Alternator

44. Altimeter

45. Amplifier

46. Amplitude

47. Analogy

48. Analysis

49. Anatomical

50. Anatomy

51. Angle of Contact

52. Angle of Deviation

53. Angle of Emergence

54. Angle of Incidence

55. Angle of Projection

56. Angle of Reflection

57. Angular Moment

58. Angular Velocity

59. Anode

60. Anticlockwise

61. Apparatus

62. Apparent

63. Apparent Expansion

64. Detergent

65. Polymer

66. Astronomical

67. Astronomy

68. Atmosphere

69. Atom

70. Atomic Number

71. Atomic Energy

72. Automatic

73. Auxiliary

74. Axis of Mirror

75. Balance Wheel

76. Balancing Point

77. Bar Magnet

78. Barograph

79. Baroscopic

80. Base

81. Battery

82. Beaker

83. Beam of Balance

84. Beam of Light

85. Beats

86. Bell Jar

87. Biconvex Lens

88. Biding Screw

89. Binding Energy

90. Bioscope

91. Black hole

92. Block

93. Boiler

94. Boiling Point

95. Boiling Point

96. Brake

97. Brush

98. Bulb

99. DNA

100. Buoyancy

101. Calculus

102. Calibration

103. Decay

104. Capacitance

105. Capillarity

106. Carbon

107. Carrier Waves

108. Cathode

109. Centrifugal

110. Centripetal

111. Chemistry

112. Chromatic Aberration

113. Chromo Sphere

114. Chronometer

115. Circulation

116. Clamp

117. Clip

118. Clockwise

119. Code

120. Coefficient

121. Accommodation

122. Cohesion

123. Collision

124. Color Blindness

125. Commutator

126. Compass

127. Compass Needle

128. Compass Points

129. Compensated

130. Compressibility

131. Computation

132. Concave

133. Concave Lens

134. Condense

135. Conductance

136. Conduction

137. Conductor

138. Conjugated Foci

139. Careless / Careful

140. Constant

141. Continuous Current

142. Convection

143. Convergent

144. Convex Lens

145. Convex Mirror

146. Core

147. Counter Clockwise

148. Counterclockwise

149. Couple

150. Couple Forces

151. Cripple

152. Crank

153. Critical Angle

154. Cross Section

155. Cross Wire

156. Cubical Expansion

157. Darkness

158. Declination

159. Definition

160. Deflection

161. Data

162. Demagnetization

163. Density

164. Detector

165. Developer

166. Development

167. Deviation

168. Dew-point

169. Diagram

170. Diaphragm

171. Diatomic scale

172. Dielectric

173. Diffraction

174. Digital

175. Dilate

176. Direct current

177. Directive property

178. Disc

179. Discord

180. Displacement

181. Divergent

182. Divisibility

183. Down stroke

184. Ductility

185. Earth

186. Ebullition

187. Eccentric

188. Efficiency

189. Effort

190. Elastic Fatigue

191. Elasticity

192. Elect

193. Electric Charge

194. Electric Circuit

195. Electric Current

196. Electric Discharge

197. Electric Field

198. Electric Induction

199. Electric Resistance

200. Electric Shock

201. Electricity

202. Electrification

203. Transformation

204. Electro Motive Force

205. Hoax

206. Electrode

207. Unscientfic

208. Electrolysis

209. Elevation

210. Electrolyte

211. Electron

212. Electronics

213. Electroscope

214. Elevator

215. Elongation

216. Emergent Ray

217. Energy

218. Engineer

219. Engineering

220. Equilibrant

221. Equilibrium

222. Exhaustion

223. Expansion

224. Eye Lens

225. Microscope

226. Fathometer

227. Fatigue

228. Film

229. Film

230. Fixed Point

231. Fixing

232. Flask

233. Flexibility

234. Flotation

235. Flow

236. Fluid

237. Focal Length

238. Focus

239. Fog

240. Force Pump

241. Formula

242. Freezing Mixture

243. Freezing Point

244. Frequency

245. Friction

246. Frictional Resistance

247. Frost

248. Fulcrum

249. Fundamental

250. Fuse

251. Gas

252. Gaseous State

253. Gauge

254. Gel

255. Generator

256. Geography

257. Geology

258. Gradual

259. Grating

260. Gravitation

261. Gravity

262. Grid

263. Hail

264. Hard

265. Hardness

266. Harmony

267. Healthy

268. Heartbeat

269. Heating effect

270. Hinge

271. Horsepower

272. Humidity

273. Hydraulic brake

274. Hydraulic press

275. Hydro meter

276. Hydrogen

277. Hygrometer

278. Hygrometric state

279. Ice

280. Ignition

281. Illuminative Power

282. Impact

283. Impulse

284. Incandescence

285. Incident Ray

286. Inclination

287. Inclined Plane

288. Incompressibility

289. Indestructibility

290. Index

291. Indigo

292. Indivisibility

293. Induction

294. Induction Coil

295. Inertia

296. Inference

297. Inflator

298. Insect

299. Insulation

300. Intensity

301. Interaction

302. Interference

303. Interval

304. Inverse Proportion

305. Invisible Rays

306. Ion

307. Ionization

308. Iridescence

309. Isothermal

310. Jet

311. Key

312. Kilogram

313. Kilowatt Hour

314. Kinematics

315. Kinetic Energy

316.   Kinetic Theory

317.   Lactometer

318.   Laser

319.   Latent Heat

320.   Lateral Displacement

321.   Lateral Inversion

322.   Lathe

323.   Law of Conservation Of Energy

324.   Law of Inertia

325.   Law of Reflection

326.   Law of Universal Gravitation

327.   Animal testing

328.   Lever

329.   Life

330.   Lifecycle

331.   Death

332.   Linear Accelerator

333.   Linear Expansion

334.   Liquefaction

335.   Liquid

336. Liquid

337. Longitudinal Wave

338. Loudness

339. Lubricant

340. A black hole

341. Solar Eclipse

342. Lunar Eclipse

343. Magic Lantern

344. Magnet

345. Moon

346. Magnetic Field

347. Magnetic Force

348. Magnetic Induction

349. Magnifying Power

350. Magnitude

351. Malleability

352. Manometer

353. Mass

354. Matter

355. Mechanics

356. Medicine

357. Medium

358. Melting Point

359. Meniscus

360. Microscope

361. Minimum Deviation

362. Mirage

363. Mist

364. Mixture

365. Momentum

366. Myopia

367. Natural Frequency

368. Net Force

369. Neutrino

370. Neutron

371. Node

372. Non-Metal

373. Normal

374. Nuclear

375. Nuclear Chain Reaction

376. Nuclear Decay Series

377. Nuclear Energy

378. Nuclear Fission

379. Nuclear Fusion

380. Nuclear Radiation

381. Nucleons

382. Nucleus

383. Nuclide

384. Objective

385. Observation

386. Octave

387. Opaque

388. Open Circuit

389. Operational Definitions

390. Optics

391. Orbital Motion

392. Ordinary Hydrogen

393. Organizing Data

394. Ort Circuit

395. Oscillation

396. Overtones

397. Oxygen

398. Parallax

399. Partial Eclipse

400. Particle

401. Pendulum

402. Penumbra

403. Pharmaceutical

404. Photometer

405. Physics

406. Physiology

407. Pitch

408. Pivot

409. Plane

410.   Plane Mirror

411. Pointer

412. Pole

413. Pollution

414. Porosity

415. Positive Electricity

416. Potential Energy

417. Potentiality

418. Power

419. Pressure

420. Principal Axis

421. Propulsion

422. Psychology

423. Pull

424. Quantized

425. Quantum

426. Quantum Mechanics

427. Quantum Number

428. Quantum of Light

429. Quantum Theory

430. Quarks

431. Radiation

432. Rain Gauge

433. Reaction

434. Reading

435. Real Image

436. Receiver

437. Recoil

438. Rectifier

439. Reflection

440. Refraction

441. Refractive Index

442. Refractometer

443. Refrigerant

444. Regulation

445. Relative Density

446. Relative Expansion

447. Relative Humidity

448. Relay

449. Repulsion

450. Reservoir

451. Resistance

452. Resolution of Forces

453. Resonance

454. Resting Point

455. Resultant

456. Retardation

457. Rigidity

458.   Rim

459.   Rocket

460.   Rotatory Compressor

461.   Rudder

462.   Safety Fuse

463.   Satellite

464.   Saturation

465.   Science

466.   Screen

467.   Screw Thread

468.   Secondary Axis

469.   Sensitized

470.   Shaft

471.   Simple Pendulum

472.   Siphon

473.   Slide Valve

474.   Slit

475.   Snow

476.   Soft

477.   Solenoid

478. Solid

479. Solidify

480. Space alien

481. Space

482. Specific Gravity

483. Specific Heat

484. Spectrometer

485. Spectroscope

486. Spectrum

487. Speed

488. Spiral Spring

489. Statics

490. Statistics

491. Universe

492. Stop Watch

493. Stopcock

494. Suction Pump

495. Suction Tube

496. Surface

497. Surface Tension

498. Swing

499. Tachometer

500. Technology

501. Telescope

502. Temperature

503. Tension

504. Terminal

505. Theory

506. Thermal capacity

507. Thermal couple

508. Thermodynamics

509. Thermostat

510. Thickness

511. Thrust

512. To bob

513. To Center

514. To create

515. To load

516. To transmit

517. Tone

518. Torsion

519.   Total internal reflection

520.   Transformer

521.   Translucent

522.   Transmitter

523.   Transparent

524.   Transverse vibration

525.   Trigonometry

526.   Tuning fork

527.   Turbine

528.   Turning point

529.   Ultimate Stress

530.   Ultrasonic

531.   Ultraviolet

532.   Unit

533.   Universe

534.   Vacuum

535.   Vacuum Brake

536.   Vacuum Tube

537.   Valve

538.   Vapor

539.   Vector

540. Vector Addition

541. Vector Resolution

542. Velocity

543. Velocity of Sound

544. Vertical Motion

545. Vibration

546. Virtual Image

547. Viscosity

548. Visible Light

549. Visible Radiation

550. Visible Spectrum

551. Vocal Chord

552. Volatile

553. Voltmeter

554. Volume

555. Water Equivalent

556. Water Level

557. Water Wheel

558. Wave

559. Ocean wave

560.   Wave Front

561.   Wave Length

562.   Wave Theory

563.   Wavelength

564.   Weak Force

565.   Weight

566.   Work Function

567.   X- Rays

568.   Zero Error Math

TECHNOLOGY VOCABULARY

569.   Application

570.   Backend

571.   Bytes

572.   Camera

573.   Certificate

574.   Change Style

575.   Commercial Use

576.   Computer storage

577.   Computer Cell

578.   Computer Virus

579.   Connection

580.   Connectivity

581.   Control Panel

582.   Control Settings

583.   Cord

584.   CPU

585.   Create

586.   Cyber

587.   Data

588.   Database

589.   Database

590.   Dead

591. Decline

592. Demand

593. Design

594. Designers

595. Detailed

596. Determine

597. Developer

598. Developers

599. Development

600. Devices

601. Digital

602. Document

603. Efficiency

604. Electronic

605. Emoji

606. Equipment

607. Expertise

608. Eyestrain

609. Font

610. Formula

611. Frontend

612. Hacking

613. Hard drive

614. Hardwire

615. Help

616. Hinge

617. Insert

618. Install

619. Internet

620. Keyboard

621. Laptop

622. Mailings

623. Mainframe

624. Memory Stick

625. Monitor

626. Non-Commercial Use

627. Optimize

628. Outsource

629. Outsourcing

630. Pad

631. Page Layout

632. Panel

633. PDF

634. Power source

635. Printers

636. Program

637. Programming

638. Region

639. Remote

640. Replace

641. Review

642. Scanner

643. Screen

644. Server

645. Settings

646. Size

647. Spyware

648. Support

649. Template

650. Tools

651. USB

652. View

653. Wi-Fi

654. Wire

655. World Wide Web (WWW)

ENGINEERING VOCABULARY

656. Absolute motion

657. Absolute pressure

658. Absolute zero

659. Absorbance

660. AC power

661. Acceleration

662. Acid

663. Acid-base reaction

664. Acoustics

665. Adhesion

666. Adiabatic process

667. Aerodynamics

668. Aerospace engineering

669. Agricultural engineering

670. Albedo

671. Algae

672. Algorithm

673. Alkane

674. Alkene

675. Alkyne

676. Alloy

677. Alpha particle

678. Alternating current

679. Alternative hypothesis

680. Amino acid

681. Amorphous solid

682. Amplitude

683. Anaerobic digestion

684. Angular acceleration

685. Angular momentum

686. Angular velocity

687. Anion

688. Annihilation

689. Anode

690. Antigravity

691. Antimatter

692. Antineutron

693. Antiparticle

694. Antiproton

695. Applied engineering

696. Arc length

697. Archimedes' principle

698. Area moment of inertia

699. Arithmetic mean

700. Arithmetic sequence

701. Aromatic hydrocarbon

702. Assembly language

703. Atom

704. Atomic mass

705. Atomic number

706. Atomic packing factor

707. Atomic physics

708. Atomic structure

709. Audio frequency

710. Automation

711. Bacteria

712. Balance sheet

713. Barometer

714. Baryon

715. Battery

716. Base

717. Baud

718. Beam

719. Bending

720. Beta particle

721. Binomial random variable

722. Biochemistry

723. Biology

724. Biomedical engineering

725. Biophysics

726. Boiling point

727. Brittle

728. Buoyancy

729. Capacitance

730. Capillarity

731. Carbonate

732. Coordinates

733. Cathode

734. Cell membrane

735. Cell nucleus

736. Cell theory

737. Center of gravity

738. Center of mass

739. Center of pressure

740. Central force motion

741. Central limit theorem

742. Central processing unit

743. Centripetal force

744. Centroid

745. Chain reaction

746. Chemical bond

747. Chemical compound

748. Equilibrium

749. Kinetics

750. Chemical reaction

751. Chemistry

752. Chloride

753. Chloroplast

754. Chromate

755. Chromosome

756. Circle

757. Circular motion

758. Civil engineering

759. Coherence

760. Cohesion

761. Compensation

762. Compiler

763. Compressive strength

764. Computer

765. Computer-aided design

766. Computer-aided engineering

767. Computer-aided manufacturing

768. Computer engineering

769. Computer science

770. Concave lens

771. Condensed matter physics

772.   Conjugate acid

773.   Conjugate base

774.   Continuum mechanics

775.   Convex lens

776.   Corrosion

777.   Cosmic rays

778.   Covalent bond

779.   Crookes tube

780.   Cryogenics

781.   Crystallization

782.   Crystallography

783.   Curvilinear motion

784.   Cyclotron

785.   Decibel

786.   Definite integral

787.   Deflection

788. Density

789. Derivative

790. Design engineering

791. Dew point

792. Differential pulley

793. Dispersion

794. Distance

795. Distance-weighted estimator

796. Doppler Effect

797. Ductility

798. Dynamics

799. Dyne

800. Economics

801. Elastic modulus

802. Elasticity

803. Electric charge

804. Electric circuit

805. Electric current

806. Electric displacement field

807. Electric generator

808. Electric field

809. Electric field gradient

810. Electric power

811. Conductor

812. Electrical insulator

813. Electrical network

814. Electrical resistance

815. Electricity

816. Electrodynamics

817. Electromagnet

818. Electromagnetic field

819. Electromagnetic radiation

820. Electron

821. Electronics

822. Energy

823. Engine

824. Engineering

825. Enzyme

826. Escape velocity

827. Exothermic

828. Fission

829. Fluid

830. Fluid mechanics

831. Fluid

832. Flywheel

833. Focus

834. Freezing point

835. Friction

836. Function

837. Fundamental frequency

838.   Fundamental interaction

839.   Fusion

840.   Gamma rays

841.   Gas

842.   Geiger counter

843.   Gluon

844.   Gravitation

845.   Gravitational constant

846.   Gravitational energy

847.   Gravitational field

848.   Gravitational potential

849.   Gravity

850.   Ground state

851.   Hadron

852.   Half-life

853.   Hardness

854. Heat transfer

855. Hertz

856. Horsepower

857. Hydraulics

858. Hydrocarbon

859. Ideal gas

860. Indefinite integral

861. Inertia

862. Infrasound

863. Integral

864. Integral transform

865. Ion

866. Ionic bond

867. Ionization

868. Inclined plane

869. Industrial engineering

870. Inorganic chemistry

871.   Isotope

872.   Laplace transform

873.   LC circuit

874.   Lepton

875.   Lever

876.   Light

877.   Linear elasticity

878.   Liquid

879.   Machine

880.   Magnetic field

881.   Magnetism

882.   Manufacturing engineering

883.   Mass balance

884.   Mass density

885.   Mass moment of inertia

886.   Mass number

887. Mass spectrometry

888. Material properties

889. Mathematics

890. Matrix

891. Matter

892. Measures of central tendency

893. Mechanical advantage

894. Mechanical engineering

895. Mechanical filter

896. Mechanical wave

897. Mechanics

898. Mechanism

899. Median

900. Melting

901. Melting point

902. Metal alloy

903. Metallic bond

904. Mode

905. Modulus of elasticity

906. Molarity

907. Molecule

908. Moment of inertia

909. Nanotechnology

910. Nuclear engineering

911. Nuclear physics

912. Nuclear potential energy

913. Nuclear power

914. Ohm

915. Optics

916. Organic chemistry

917. Osmosis

918. Parallel circuit

919. Paraffin

920. Particle accelerator

921. Particle displacement

922. Pendulum

923. Petrol

924. Photon

925. Physical chemistry

926. Physical quantity

927. Physics

928. Planck constant

929. Plasma physics

930. Plasticity

931. Power

932. Pressure

933. Probability

934. Quantum mechanics

935. Quantum physics

936. Regelation

937. Relative density

938. Robotics

939. Rotational energy

940. Rotational speed

941. Shear strength

942. Shortwave radiation

943. Simple machine

944. Solubility

945. Sound

946. Special relativity

947. Specific heat

948. Specific gravity

949. Specific volume

950. Specific weight

951. Spontaneous combustion

952. State of matter

953. Statics

954. Statistics

955. Strain

956. Strain hardening

957. Strength of materials

958. Sublimation

959. Surcharge

960. Surface tension

961. Superconductor

962. Technical standard

963. Temperature

964. Tensile force

965. Tension member

966. Thermal conduction

967. Thermal equilibrium

968. Thermal radiation

969. Thermodynamics

970. Theory of relativity

971. Torque

972. Toughness

973. Trajectory

974. Transducer

975. Trigonometry

976. Uncertainty principle

977. Unicode

978. Unit vector

979. Unsaturated compound

980. Utility frequency

981. Vacuole

982. Vacuum

983. Valence

984. Valence band

985. Valence electron

986.   Valence shell

987.   Valve

988.   Vector space

989.   Vibration

990.   Viscosity

991.   Volt-ampere

992.   Volt-ampere reactive

993.   Wave

994.   Wavelength

995.   Wedge

996.   Weighted mean

997.   Wheel and axle

MATHEMATICS VOCABULARY

998.   Abscissa

999. Absolute

1000. Absolute value

1001. Add to

1002. Addition

1003. Adjacent

1004. Algebra

1005. Alternate

1006. Altitude

1007. Angle

1008. Antiderivatives

1009. Approximately

1010. Arc

1011. Arcs

1012. Axis

1013. Balance a Checkbook

1014. Base

1015. Bisect

1016. Budget

1017. Calculator

1018. Calculus

1019. Capacity

1020. Cardinal Number

1021. Celsius

1022. Circles

1023. Classification

1024. Combine

1025. Complementary

1026. Complex numbers

1027. Composite Numbers

1028. Computer memory

1029. Concurrent

1030. Cone

1031. Congruent triangle

1032. Consecutive

1033. Constant

1034. Construct

1035. Continuity

1036. Conversions

1037. Coordinate plane

1038. Corresponding

1039. Cube root

1040. Currency

1041. Decimal

1042. Decrease

1043. Deduction

1044. Denominator

1045. Diagonal line

1046. Diameter

1047. Difference between

1048. Division

1049. Dot paper

1050. Ellipse

1051. Equality

1052. Equals

1053. Equilateral

1054. Estimate

1055. Even number

1056. Exchange

1057. Exponent

1058. Express

1059. Exterior

1060. Factor

1061. Factor tree

1062. Fahrenheit

1063. Fewer

1064. Figures, Tables and Charts

1065. Financial interest

1066. Finite

1067. Formula

1068. Fraction

1069. Geometry

1070. Graph

1071. Graph paper

1072. Greatest Common Factor

1073. Height

1074. Horizontal line

1075. Hyperbola

1076. Improper

1077. Increase

1078. Inequality

1079. Integer

1080. Integer

1081. Intensity

1082. Iota

1083. Irrational Number

1084. Isometric

1085. Least Common Factor

1086. Length

1087. Less

1088. Limits

1089. Linear Equation

1090. Logarithmic Function

1091. Math Vocabulary

1092. Matrices

1093. Maximum

1094. Measures

1095. Meter

1096. Metric

1097. Minus

1098. Multiple

1099. Multiplication

1100. Multiplication table

1101. Negative

1102. Net

1103. Notation

1104. Numbers

1105. Numeral

1106. Numerator

1107. Obtuse

1108. Octagon

1109. Odd

1110. Odds

1111. Order of operations

1112. Ordinal Number

1113. Parabola

1114. Patterns

1115. Percent

1116. Percent

1117. Permutations

1118. Perpendicular lines

1119. Pi

1120. Plot

1121. Plotting points

1122. Polygon

1123. Prime Numbers

1124. Probability

1125. Product of

1126. Proofs

1127. Proportion

1128. Protractor

1129. Pyramid

1130. Quadrant

1131. Quadrant

1132. Quotient

1133. Radius

1134. Ratio

1135. Ration

1136. Rational Number

1137. Real Number

1138. Reciprocal

1139. Rectangle

1140. Right

1141. Roman Number

1142. Rule

1143. Ruler

1144. Scale

1145. Scientific

1146. Segment

1147. Simplest

1148. Simplify

1149. Square

1150. Square Root

1151. Strategies

1152. Subtraction

1153. Sum

1154. Supplementary

1155. Symbols

1156. Tangent

1157. Tangram

1158. Temperature

1159. Tessellations

1160. Tetrahedron

1161. Theorem

1162. Total

1163. Transversal

1164. Triangle

1165. Trigonometry

1166. Union

1167. Unit of Measurement

1168. Variable

1169. Variation

1170. Vector

1171. Vertical

1172. Vertical line

1173. Volume

1174. Weights

1175. Whole Number

1176. Width

1177. Yard stick

===

===

===

===

===

===

NOTES

NOTES

NOTES

NOTES

NOTES

NOTES

NOTES

NOTES

NOTES

===

===

===

===

===

===

===

===

                                        =================================

CHARTS DEFINITION

WORD	DEFINITION

CHARTS DEFINITION

WORD	DEFINITION

===

===

===

===

===

===

===

                                        =====================================

CHARTS DEFINITION

WORD	DEFINITION

CHARTS DEFINITION

WORD	DEFINITION

=====================================

=====================================

=====================================

=====================================

=====================================

CHARTS DEFINITION

WORD	DEFINITION

CHARTS DEFINITION

WORD	DEFINITION

==

===

CHARTS DEFINITION

WORD	DEFINITION

CHARTS DEFINITION

WORD	DEFINITION

CHARTS DEFINITION

WORD	DEFINITION

==

==

==

==

==

==

==

==

                                        ==

CHARTS DEFINITION

WORD	DEFINITION

CHARTS DEFINITION

WORD	DEFINITION

===

===

===

===

===

                                    =====================================

CHARTS DEFINITION

WORD	DEFINITION

CHARTS DEFINITION

WORD	DEFINITION

==

==

==

==

CHARTS DEFINITION

WORD	DEFINITION

CHARTS DEFINITION

WORD	DEFINITION

==

==

CHARTS DEFINITION

WORD	DEFINITION

CHARTS DEFINITION

WORD	DEFINITION

CHARTS DEFINITION

WORD	**DEFINITION**

CHARTS DEFINITION

WORD	DEFINITION

CHARTS DEFINITION

WORD	DEFINITION

Christine Canning Wilson / STEM ESL Arabic

الإنجليزية، جدول محتويات

- القسم الأول: الأفعال تعليمات الفصل الدراسي لوقف على أساس دورة العمل
-
- القسم الثاني: العلوم المفردات
- القسم الثالث: التكنولوجيا والكمبيوتر المفردات
- القسم الرابع: المفردات الهندسية
- القسم الخامس: مفردات الرياضيات

الجزء الثاني: الترجمة العربية

الجزء الثالث: مجال دراسة الطالب

الكلمات الإنجليزية الأساسية المستخدمة في العلوم والتكنولوجيا، والهندسة والرياضيات

من أجل

متعلمي اللغة الإنجليزية

هامة: وقد "اللغة الإنجليزية" أكثر من الكلمات من اللغة الخاصة بك. قد لا تكون بعض الكلمات ترجمة. بعض الكلمات تقرب. بعض الكلمات هي نفس الكلمة باللغة الإنجليزية. هذا الكتاب دليل فقط. وسوف تساعدك على الحصول على الإنصاف للمناهج الدراسية. تطابق العدد في اللغة الخاصة بك مع عدد المستخدمة في "قسم اللغة الإنجليزية". طلب المساعدة من المعلم الخاص بك.

قوائم مفردات اللغة الإنجليزية

الفصول الدراسية تعليم الأفعال المستخدمة في العلوم والتكنولوجيا والهندسة والرياضيات

1- استيعاب

2- تسريع

3- عمل

4- إضافة

5- قم بمحاذاة

6- تضخيم

7- تحليل

8-جواب

9. إرفاق

10. التوازن

11-جلب

12-لتغيير

13-كاملة

14-حساب

15-ثابت

16-تحويل

17-العد

18-إنقاص

19-وصف

20-تحديد

21-استنباط

22-التفريق بين

23-تمييع

24-يزيح

25-لا تلمس

26-السحب

27- هندسة

28-الهروب

29-دراسة

30- التجربة

31- تتطور

32. إصلاح

33. اتبع

34. كسر

35. التعامل برفق

36. الغراء

37. تنمو

38. تخمين

39. الحرارة

40. مرفاع

41. عقد

42. غير مكتملة

43. زيادة

44. دمج

45- ترك

46. رفع

47. رفع

48. الاستماع

49. السفلي

50. التدبير

51. ميكس

52. ضرب

53. إشعار

54. مراقبة

55. ترتيب

56. شريك

57- مكان

58. من أجل

59- ويحظر

60. رتبة

61- التموينية

62. الجنيه

63. إزالة

64. رد الفعل

65. قراءة

66. إزالة

67. استبدال

68. تقرير

69. تدوير

70- تشبع

71. العلوم

الأشكال المستخدمة في العلوم والتكنولوجيا، والهندسة والرياضيات

1- أنبوب

2- المثلث

3- اسطوانة

4- كهف

5- القوس

6- دائرة

7- ساحة

8- مستطيل

9. شكل بيضوي

10. على شكل قلب

11- تذبذب

12- دائرية

13- مموج

14- عثرة

15- اثنين الأبعاد

16- ثلاثة الأبعاد

17- مسطح

18- جولة

19- مخروط

20- الموازية

21- المتاخمة

22- الشق

مفردات العلوم

23- مشروع العلوم

24- انحراف

25- المطلقة

26- الطاقة الاستيعابية

27- تسريع

69.ذرة

70ـ العدد الذري

71. الطاقة الذرية

72. التلقائي

73. مساعدة

74. محور لمرآة

75. عجلة التوازن

76ـ موازنة نقطة

77. شريط مغناطيس

78. باروجراف

79. باروسكوبيك

80. قاعدة

81. البطارية

82. الكأس

83. شعاع من التوازن

84. شعاع من الضوء

85. يدق

86ـ جرة بيل

87. عدسة بيكونفيكس

88. المتعهدة المسمار

110. المركزي

111. الكيمياء

112. زيغ

113. المجال كرومو

114. الكرونومتر

115. الدورة الدموية

116. المشبك

117. قصاصة

118. عكس اتجاه عقارب الساعة

119. التعليمات البرمجية

120. معامل

121. أماكن السكن

122. التماسك

123. الاصطدام

124. عمي الألوان

125. مبدلة

126. بوصلة

127. إبرة البوصلة

128. نقاط البوصلة

129. تعويض

191.مرونة

192. انتخاب

193. الشحنة الكهربائية

194. الدارة الكهربائية

195. التيار الكهربائي

196.تفريغ كهربائي

197. المجال الكهربائي

198. الحث الكهربائي

199.مقاومة كهربائية

200-صدمة كهربائية

201.الكهرباء

202-كهربة

203.التحول

204.القوة المحركة الكهربائية

205.خدعة

206.قطب كهربائي

207.أونسسينتفيك

208.التحليل الكهربائي

209.ارتفاع

311.مفتاح

312.كيلوغرام

313.كيلوواط/ساعة

314.الكينماتيكا

315.الطاقة الحركية

316.النظرية الحركية

317.لاكتوميتير

318.ليزر

319.الحرارة الكامنة

320.تشريد الأفقي

321.انعكاس أفقي

322.مخرطة

323.قانون حفظ الطاقة

324.قانون القصور الذاتي

325.قانون الانعكاس

326.قانون الجاذبية العالمية

327.حيوان اختبار

328.رافعة

329.الحياة

330-دورة حياة

474. الشق

475. سنو

476. لينة

477. الملف اللولبي

478. الصلبة

479. يصلب

480. الفضاء الغريبة

481. الفضاء

482. الثقل النوعي

483. الحرارة النوعية

484. مطياف

485. المطياف

486. الطيف

487. السرعة

488. دوامة الربيع

489. إحصائيات

490. إحصائيات

491. الكون

492. وقف يشاهد

493. محبس الحنفية

494. مضخة شفط

495. أنبوب الشفط

496. السطح

497. التوتر السطحي

498. أرجوحة

499. مقياس سرعة الدوران

500- التكنولوجيا

501. تلسكوب

502. درجة الحرارة

503. التوتر

504. المحطة الطرفية

505. نظرية

506. القدرة الحرارية

507. زوجين الحرارية

508. الديناميكا الحرارية

509. الحرارة

510. سمك

511. التوجه

512. لبوب

513. إلى مركز

514. لإنشاء

515. لتحميل

516. أحيل

517. نغمة

518. فتل

519. الانعكاس الداخلي الكلي

520. محول

521. شبه شفاف

522. جهاز الإرسال

523. شفافة

524. اهتزاز عرضية

525. علم المثلثات

526. شوكة رنانة

527. عنفه

528. نقطة تحول

529. الإجهاد في نهاية المطاف

530. بالموجات فوق الصوتية

531. الأشعة فوق البنفسجية.

532. وحدة

533. الكون

534. الفراغ

555. المياه ما يعادل

556. مستوى المياه

557. عجلة الماء

558. موجه

559. أمواج المحيطات

560. جبهة الموجه

561. طول الموجه

562. نظرية الموجه

563. الطول الموجي

564. قوة الضعفاء

565. الوزن

566. وظيفة عمل

567. أشعة X

568. خطأ في الرياضيات صفر

مفردات التكنولوجيا

595. مفصلة

596. تحديد

597. المطور

598. المطورين

599. التنمية

600. الأجهزة

601. الرقمية

602. الوثيقة

603. الكفاءة

604. الإلكترونية

605. Emoji

606. المعدات

607. الخبرة الفنية

608. إجهاد العين

609. الخط

610. الصيغة

611. الواجهة الأمامية

612. القرصنة

613. محرك الأقراص الصلبة

614. يربط

615. مساعدة

616. المفصلي

617. إدراج

618. تثبيت

619. شبكة الإنترنت

620. لوحة المفاتيح

621. أجهزة الكمبيوتر المحمول

622. مراسلات

623. الحاسوب الكبير

624. عصا الذاكرة

625. مراقب

626. الاستخدام غير التجاري

627. الأمثل

628. الاستعانة بمصادر خارجية

629. الاستعانة بمصادر خارجية

630. وسادة

631. تخطيط الصفحة

632. لوحة

633. قوات الدفاع الشعبي

634.مصدر الطاقة

635. الطابعات

636. البرنامج

637.برمجة

638.المنطقة

639. البعيد

640. استبدال

641. استعراض

642. الماسح الضوئي

643. الشاشة

644. خادم

645. إعدادات

646. الحجم

647. برامج التجسس

648. الدعم

649. قالب

650. أدوات

651. الناقل التسلسلي العام

652. طريقة العرض

653. وأي فأي

654. أسلاك

655. World Wide Web (WWW)

المفردات الهندسية

656. الحركة المطلقة

657. الضغط المطلق

671. الطحالب

672. خوارزمية

673. ألكان

674. الكين

675. ألكاين

676. سبيكة

677. جسيمات ألفا

678. التيار المتردد

679. الفرضية البديلة

680. حمض أميني

681. أمورفوس الصلبة

682. السعة

683. الهضم اللاهوائي

684. التسارع الزاوي

685. زخم زاوي

686. السرعة الزاوية

687. انيون

688. الفناء

689. الأنود

690. مضاد الجاذبية

691. المادة المضادة

692. أنتينيوترون

693. أنتيبارتيكلي

694. نقيض البروتون

695. الهندسة التطبيقية

696. طول القوس

710. التشغيل الآلي للمكاتب

711. البكتيريا

712. الميزانية العمومية

713. بارومتر

714. باريون

715. البطارية

716. قاعدة

717. سرعة البث بالباود

718. شعاع

719. الانحناء

720. جسيمات بيتا

721. متغير عشوائي ثنائي الحد

722. الكيمياء الحيوية

723. علم الأحياء

724. الهندسة الطبية الحيوية

725. الفيزياء الحيوية

726. نقطة الغليان

727. هش

728. قابلية الطفو

729. السعة

730. الشعرية

731. كربونات

732. وتنسق

733. الكاثود

734. غشاء الخلية

735. نواة الخلية

736. نظرية الخلية

737. مركز الجاذبية

738. مركز الكتلة

739. مركز للضغط

740. القوة المركزية للحركة

741. مبرهنة الحد المركزية

742. وحدة المعالجة المركزية

743. قوة الجاذبية

744. Centroid

745. سلسلة من ردود الفعل

746. الرابطة الكيميائية

747. مركب كيميائي

748. التوازن

749. حركية

750. تفاعل كيميائي

751. الكيمياء

752. كلوريد

753. بلاستيدات الخضراء

754. كرومات

755. كروموسوم

756. دائرة

757. حركة دائرية

758. الهندسة المدنية

759. التماسك

760. التماسك

761. التعويض

762. برنامج التحويل البرمجي

763. قوة ضاغطة

764. جهاز الكمبيوتر

765. التصميم بمساعدة الحاسوب

766. هندسة الحاسوب

767. التصنيع بمساعدة الحاسوب

768. هندسة الحاسوب

769. علوم الحاسب الآلي

770. عدسة مقعرة

771. مكثف يهم الفيزياء

772. حمض مترافق

773. متزاوجة قاعدة

774. ميكانيكا استمرارية

775. عدسة كونفكس

776. التآكل

777. الأشعة الكونية

778. رابطة تساهمية

779. أنبوب Crookes

780. فيزياء درجات الحرارة المتدنية

781. تبلور

782. علم البلورات

783. الحركة المنحنية الخطوط

784. سيكلوترون

785. ديسيبل

786. متكاملة محددة

787. انحراف

814. مقاومة كهربائية

815. الكهرباء

816. الديناميكا الكهربائية

817. مغناطيس

818. المجال الكهرومغناطيسي

819. الإشعاع الكهرومغناطيسي

820. إلكترون

821. إلكترونيات

822. الطاقة

823. محرك

824. الهندسة

825. إنزيم

826. سرعة الإفلات

827. طارد

828. الأنشطار

829. السوائل

830. ميكانيكا الموائع

831. السوائل

832. دولاب الموازنة

833. التركيز

834. نقطة التجمد

835. الاحتكاك

836. الدالة

837. التردد الأساسي

838. التفاعل الأساسية

839. الانصهار

840. أشعة غاما

841. الغاز

842. عداد غايغر

843. غلوون

844. الجاذبية

845. ثابت الجاذبية

846. الطاقة الجاذبية

847. حقل الجاذبية

848. الجاذبية المحتملة

849. الجاذبية

850. أرض الدولة

851. هادرون

852. نصف العمر

853. صلابة

854. نقل الحرارة

855. هيرتز

856. حصان

857. الهيدروليكية

858. النفط والغاز

859. الغاز المثالي

860. متكامل محدد

861. القصور الذاتي

862. دون الصوتية

863. لا يتجزأ

864. تحويل متكاملة

865. أيون

866. رابطة أيونية

867. التأين

868. الطائرة تميل

869. الهندسة الصناعية

870. الكيمياء اللاعضوية

871. النظائر

872. تحويل لابلاس

873. الدارة LC

874. يبتون

875. رافعة

876. الضوء

877. مرونة خطية

878. سائل

879. آلة

880. المجال المغناطيسي

881. المغناطيسية

882. الهندسة الصناعية

883. توازن الكتلة

884. كثافة الكتلة

885. كتلة لحظة من الجمود

886. عدد الكتلة

887. قياس الطيف الكتلي

888. خصائص المواد

889. الرياضيات

890. مصفوفة

891. هذه المسألة

892. مقاييس النزعة المركزية

893. الميزة الميكانيكية

894. الهندسة الميكانيكية

895. عامل التصفية الميكانيكية

896. موجه ميكانيكية

897. ميكانيكا

898. إليه

899. الوسيط

900. ذوبان

901. نقطة الانصهار

902. سبيكة معدنية

903. بوند معدني

904. وضع

905. معامل مرونة

906. مولاريتي

907. جزيء

908. لحظة من الجمود

909. تقنية النانو

910. الهندسة النووية

911. الفيزياء النووية

912. طاقة نووية

913. الطاقة النووية

914. أوم

915. بصريات

916. الكيمياء العضوية

917. التناضح

918.دارة موازية

919. البارافين

920.مسرع الجسيمات

921. التشرد الجسيمات

922.رقاص

923. البنزين

924.فوتون

925.كيمياء فيزيائية

926. الكمية الفعلية

927. الفيزياء

928.ثابت بلانك

929.فيزياء البلازما

930.اللدونة

944. القابلية للذوبان

945. الصوت

946. نظرية النسبية الخاصة

947. الحرارة النوعية

948. الثقل النوعي

949. وحدة التخزين المحددة

950. الوزن النوعي

951. الاحتراق التلقائي

952. الدولة لهذه المسألة

953. إحصائيات

954. إحصائيات

955. سلالة

956. تصلب سلالة

957. قوة المواد

958. التسامي

959. لقاء تكلفة إضافية

960. التوتر السطحي

961. سوبركندوكتور

962. المعيار التقني

963. درجة الحرارة

964. قوة الشد

965- الأعضاء التوتر

966. التوصيل الحراري

967. التوازن الحراري

968. الإشعاع الحراري

969. الديناميكا الحرارية

970. نظرية النسبية

971. عزم الدوران

972. المتانة

973. مسار

974- محول طاقة

975. علم المثلثات

976. مبدأ عدم اليقين

977. يونيكود

978. متجه الوحدة

979. مجمع أونساتوراتيد

980. الأداة المساعدة للتردد

981. المنقبضة

982. الفراغ

996. يعني المرجح

997. العجلة المحور

مفردات الرياضيات

998. الاحداثي السيني

999. المطلقة

1000. القيمة المطلقة

1001. إضافة إلى

1002. إضافة

1003. المتاخمة

1004. الجبر

1005. البديل

1006. علو

1007. زاوية

1008. أنتيديريفاتيفيس

1009. حوالي الساعة

1032. على التوالي

1033. ثابت

1034. بناء

1035. الاستمرارية

1036. التحويلات

1037. تنسيق الطائرة

1038. المقابلة

1039. جذر المكعب

1040. تحويل العملات

1041. عشري

1042. إنقاص

1043. خصم

1044. قاسم

1045. خط قطري

1046. قطر

1047. الفرق بين

1048. شعبة

1049. ورقة دوت

1050. القطع الناقص

1051. المساواة

1052. يساوي

1053. متساوي الأضلاع

1054. تقدير

1055. عدد زوجي

1056. تبادل

1057. الأس

1058. نعرب عن

1059. الخارجي

1060. عامل

1061. شجرة عامل

1062. فهرنهايت

1063. أقل

1064. الأرقام والجداول والرسوم البيانية

1065. الفائدة المالية

1066. المحدودة

1067. الصيغة

1068. كسر

1069. هندسة

1070. الرسم البياني

1071. ورقة الرسم البياني

1072. العامل المشترك الأكبر

1073. الارتفاع

1074. الخط الأفقي

1075. القطع الزائد

1076. غير لائق

1077. زيادة

1078. عدم المساواة

1079. عدد صحيح

1080. عدد صحيح

1081. كثافة

1082. ايوتا

1083. عدد الطائشة

1084. متساوي القياس

1085. العوامل الأقل شيوعاً

1086. طول

1087. أقل

1088. حدود

1089. معادلة خطية

1090. الدالة اللوغاريتمية

1091. مفردات الرياضيات

1092. المصفوفات

1093. الحد الأقصى

1094. التدابير

1095. متر

1096. متري

1097. ناقص

1098. متعددة

1099. الضرب

1100. جدول الضرب

1101. السلبية

1102. صافي

1103. تدوين

1104. أرقام

1105. الأرقام

1106. البسط

1107. منفرجة

1108. المثمن

1109. الغريب

1110. الصعاب

1111. ترتيب العمليات

1112. عدد ترتيبي

1113. قطع مكافئ

1114. أنماط

1115. في المائة

1116. في المائة

1117. التباديل

1118. خطين متعامدين

1119. Pi

1120. ارسم

1121. رسم النقاط

1122. مضلع

1123. أرقام رئيس الوزراء

1124. الاحتمال

1125. المنتج من

1126. البراهين

1127. نسبة

1128. منقلة

1129. هرم

1130. رباعي،

1131. رباعي،

1132. حاصل قسمة

1133. دائرة نصف قطرها

1134. نسبة

1135. التموينية

1136. عدد الرشيد

1137. عدد حقيقي

1138. المعاملة بالمثل

1161. مبرهنة

1162. المجموع

1163. مستعرضة

1164. المثلث

1165. علم المثلثات

1166. الاتحاد

1167. وحدة القياس

1168. متغير

1169. تباين

1170. مكافحة ناقلات

1171. عمودي

1172. خط عمودي

1173. وحدة التخزين

1174. الأوزان

1175. عدد صحيح

1176. العرض

1177. عصا يارد

وتلاحظ

===

===

===

===

===

===

===

===

===

===

===

===

===

===

===

===

===

                                    =================================

وتلاحظ

===

===

===

وتلاحظ

وتلاحظ

وتلاحظ

==

==

==

==

تعريف المخططات

كلمة	تعريف	

==

==

<h2 style="text-align:center">تعريف المخططات</h2>

كلمة	تعريف

==

==

تعريف المخططات

كلمة	تعريف	

تعريف المخططات

كلمة	تعريف	

تعريف المخططات

كلمة	تعريف	

===

===

===

===

ESL – Glossary Edition: English-Arabic

===

===

===

===

===

===

===

===

                                        ==

تعريف المخططات

تعريف	كلمة

تعريف المخططات

كلمة	تعريف

==

==

==

==

==

                                    ==

تعريف المخططات

كلمة	تعريف

==

==

==

==

                                    ==

تعريف المخططات

كلمة	تعريف	

Christine Canning Wilson / STEM ESL Arabic

==

==

==

                                    ==

تعريف المخططات

كلمة	تعريف	

==

==

تعريف المخططات

كلمة	تعريف

==

                                    ==

تعريف المخططات

كلمة	تعريف

تعريف المخططات

كلمة	تعريف

تعريف المخططات

كلمة	تعريف	

===

===

===

===

==

==

==

==

==

==

==

                                   ==

تعريف المخططات

تعريف	كلمة

تعريف المخططات

كلمة	تعريف	

==

==

==

==

==

                                                    ==

تعريف المخططات

كلمة	تعريف

تعريف المخططات

كلمة	تعريف	

Christine Canning Wilson / STEM ESL Arabic

==

==

==

                            ==

تعريف المخططات

كلمة	تعريف	

===

===

تعريف المخططات

كلمة	تعريف

Christine Canning-Wilson /د. كريستين تعليب ويلسون

تدرس كريستين تعليب ويلسون في جامعة الإمارات العربية المتحدة، كلية أبوظبي للطلاب في كليات التقنية العليا، وCERT في دولة الإمارات العربية المتحدة. هي معلم مرخص والمسؤول. أنها كسبت 5 درجات الجامعة بما في ذلك ESOL واللغات الأجنبية. وقد حصلت على العديد من الجوائز. انها بتدريب المعلمين والطلاب في جميع أنحاء العالم.

Christine Canning-Wilson taught at United Arab Emirates University, Abu Dhabi Men's College at the Higher Colleges of Technology, and CERT in the United Arab Emirates. She is a licensed teacher and administrator. She has earned 5 University degrees including ESOL and foreign languages. She has won many awards. She trains teachers and students worldwide.

CPSIA information can be obtained
at www.ICGtesting.com
Printed in the USA
LVOW03s1546191115

463343LV00010B/579/P